First published by Zidane Press i

Copyright © by Richard Osborne
Illustrations © by Georgia Harriso

All rights reserved.
Zidane Press Ltd.
19 Tremlet Grove,
London N19 3UH

Design by Greg Tilley

Distributed by:
Turnaround Publisher Services Ltd.
Unit 3
Olympia Trading Estate
London N2Z 6TZ

T: +44 (0)20 8829 3019

ISBN 0–95484–213–8

Richard Osborne is the author of many internationally best-selling
works in the humanities and social sciences including *Philosophy for
Beginners*, *Freud for Beginners*, *Megawords* (Sage), *Sociology for
Beginners* and recently, *The Universe*.

His forthcoming work *Art Theory for Beginners* will be published by
Zidane Press in May 2006.

Greg Tilley, **Georgia Harrison** and **Claire Softley** are all designers
or illustrators living and working in London.

KANT'S VERY LARGE MORALITY HANDBOOK

POCKET
HEDGEHOGS

4

Morality is a matter of right and wrong, good and bad. So, what could be simpler? If you are a fundamentalist Christian, Muslim or Jew (or anything else) there is no problem. You do what the prophet, God or whoever tells you. However even that can be tricky because the evidence isn't always clear, sometimes in the bible God says things like 'smite all your enemies with a big sword' when they annoy you, which we mostly don't accept anymore.

So how do you decide what is moral, what is right or wrong. Philosophers have had a good deal to say about all of this and no-one more than Kant, the great eighteenth century thinker. He believed that there were moral absolutes, that is rules that were unchanging about how to be good but lots of people have disagreed with that.

This last century the basis of moral thinking has become very much more complex as a lot of people don't believe in a God or some other abstract being to decide things. The way we live has got more complicated as well so that what used to seem like simple questions, like who's your father, can get very messy.

Technology and social change have put real strain on what people think is right and wrong, for example lots of people now think that is justifiable to do anything to get on television. Funnily enough God didn't have much to say about television he only ever went on about sheep and cattle and your neighbour's ass, so there's not much help from the bible.

There is the law to tell you what's right and wrong but that has it's limits as well, like the law says you can't smoke cannabis but you can drink yourself stupid and smoke tobacco till you fall off the perch. Anyway what is legal and what is moral probably aren't the same thing. In this book we have selected many different philosopher's approaches to moral questions to show you how difficult it can be to be sure that you are doing the right thing. (Or perhaps the wrong thing for the right reason).

Morality is either:
a) A code of conduct put forward by society
b) or religion (or group)
c) Made up by individuals.
d) Something all rational people adhere to.
e) A means of justifying almost anything.

RICH PEOPLE HAVE MORALS,
POOR PEOPLE HAVE DEBTS.
(ANON)

Morality is a universal law, hidden only by human confusion.
— Rothka

Morality in general is a really difficult thing, and the more you think about it the less obvious it appears. Being moral supposedly means telling the difference between right and wrong, if it was that simple we'd all be moral. Some modern critics argue that morality stinks of self-righteousness, or fear, not of loving thy neighbour. Perhaps being moral is like being popular, its great while the feeling lasts, but it wears off and actually it was always just being selfish. This is to say that being moral is quite often just being smug and pretending to behave better than other people.

One man's morality is, in other words, another woman's bad behaviour, or someone else's best behaviour. Sin is in the eyes of the wicked, who come eyeball to eyeball with lust...

Being good is like being dead only more boring...
— W. Miller

If you think about it immorality is a longer and more interesting word than morality. Where there are laws to govern things it always seems like more fun to go against the rules. In the jungle, as they say, the law of the jungle operates, and this means that the survival of the fittest seems to be the main rule. We, however, as humans are supposed to be above the laws of the jungle, but that may be because we don't understand them.

Or as Kant said "I have no knowledge of myself as I am, but merely as I appear to myself". So if I don't know who I am I can hardly be blamed for misbehaving. Thus morality is always about someone else.

HERE ARE WHAT SOME **MAJOR** PHILOSOPHERS HAVE HAD TO SAY ABOUT MORALITY.

FIRST OF ALL, KANT, THE GREAT MORALIST:

It is only as a moral being that man can be a final purpose of creation.

Two things fill the mind with ever new and increasing admiration and awe, the oftener and more steadily we reflect on them: the starry heavens above and the moral law within.

We do not need science and philosophy to know what we should do to be honest and good, yea, even wise and virtuous.

The majesty of duty has nothing to do with the enjoyment of life.

AND HIS MAJOR LAW ON HOW MORALITY FUNCTIONS:

There is therefore but one categorical imperative, namely this: act only on that maxim whereby thou canst at the same time will that it should become a universal law.

This sort of means only do things that generally seem to be right! (to be imprecisely vague)

And at the other end of the spectrum we have the great debunker of all religious morality Frederich Nietzsche, the nihilist & several of his friends:

"Obedience" and "Law" that is what hears in all moral sentiments. But "Caprice" and "Freedom" might yet be the last sound that morality makes in the end.
— Friedrich Nietzsche

In morality, man treats himself not as individuum but as dividuum.
— Friedrich Nietzsche

Every word is a prejudice.

Error has transformed animals into men; could truth be capable of transforming man again into animal.

Morality is always the product of terror, its chains and straight coats are fashioned by those who dare not trust others because they dare not trust themselves to walk freely.
— Aldous Huxley

Morality is simply the attitude we adopt towards people we personally dislike.
— Oscar Wilde

Morality is a burglars tool whose merit lies in never being left behind at the scene of the crime.
— Karl Krause

There ought to be limits to freedom.
— G.W. Bush

This would be a hell of a lot easier if it was a dictatorship.
— G.W. Bush

I'm not the expert on how the Iraqi people think, because
I live in America, where it's nice and safe and secure.
— G.W. Bush (Sep. 23 2004)

The people get the government they deserve.
— De Tocqueville

FOR PHILOSOPHERS

If only those actions are moral, which are performed out
of freedom of will, then there are no moral actions.
— F. Nietzsche.

To wish to be better than the world is already to be on the
threshold of immorality.
— Bradley. F.H.

I had rather be mad than moral, then I would have no
knowledge of my wrong-doing.
— Bernard Stone.

It is not the community's morality that counts, but what
counts as the community 's morality.
— Richard Rorty.

Or in fact morality is simply man's desire to elucidate the universal. So is God moral? Morality is what distinguishes us from animals, which is presumably why we kill them for pleasure.

CHRISTIANITY

Your love of your neighbour is your bad love of
yourselves.
— Nietzsche, F.

(By which Fredrich was implying that Christianity was
all about lack of self-awareness, and self-respect)

It is only as a moral being that man can be a final purpose
of creation.
— Kant, I.

(One of the stronger underlying ideas in Kant's
philosophy)

Forgiveness, rather than revenge, is the final irony of
religion. Christianity is no more than the mechanisation
of platonic ideals, middle-eastern fluidity and
Scandinavian guilt. (all religions are pastiches of one
another – that's why they all hate each other!)

Suffer then my forgiving as I forgive your suffering.

THE CHURCH AND MORALITY

In this soulless and cynical age its harder than ever to act morally. The post modem sensibility means that anything goes, that there are no objective laws. Where and to whom do we look in this moral vacuum? How can we raise decent children? What is our last chance for salvation, our unwavering rock of ages? Politicians? The justice system? Television? Its all very confusing, so look to the Church. It'll tell you what to think.

HOW TO DEAL WITH DYSFUNCTIONAL KIDS

"Anyone who curses his father or mother must be put to death."
— Jesus — Matthew 15:4

If a man have a stubborn and rebellious son. . . then shall
his father and mother. . . bring him out unto the elders of
the city.. . And all the men shall stone him with stones,
that he die
— Deuteronomy 21: 18-21

Some small boys came out of the city and jeered at the
prophet Elisha saying "Go up you baldhead! Go up you
baldhead!" And he cursed them in the name of the Lord.
And two she bears came out of the woods and tore forty
two of the boys.
— 11 Kings 2:23-24

TREATMENT OF WOMEN

"Now kill all the boys. And kill every woman who has slept with a man, but save for yourselves every girl who has never slept with a man.."
— Numbers 31:32-35

It is disgraceful for a woman to speak in the church
— Corinthians 14:33-35

A woman should learn quietness and full submission. I do
not permit a woman to teach or to have authority over a
man; she must be silent
— Timothy 2:9-14

Women are naturally, morally and religiously defective.
(Bukhary) Hadith.

A FEW WORDS FROM THE PRINCE OF PEACE .....

"... Those enemies of mine who do not want me to be king over them, bring them here and kill them in front of me "
— Jesus — Luke 19:26-27

"Do not suppose that I have come to bring peace to the earth. I did not come to bring peace, but a sword. For I have come to turn a man against his father, a daughter against her mother, a daughter in law against a mother in law. A man's enemies will be the members of his own household."
— Matthew 10:37-38

It is easy to have a friend, but a follower of Jesus has to love an enemy as well.
— Matthew 5:38-48

AND SOME WORDS OF TOLERANCE FROM THE VATICAN

... according to the objective moral order homosexual relations are acts which lack an essential and indispensable finality. In scripture they are condemned as serious depravity. . . intrinsically disordered and in no case be approved.

Masturbation is an intrinsically and seriously disordered act... whatever the motive for acting in this way, the deliberate use of the sexual faculty outside of normal conjugal relations essentially contradicts the finality of the faculty. It lacks the sexual relationship called for by the moral order

SOME DIFFERING VIEWS ON THE
SUBJECTS OF CHRISTIANITY
FAITH AND MORALITY....

All religions begin with a revolt against morality, and
perish when morality conquers them"
— George Bernard Shaw

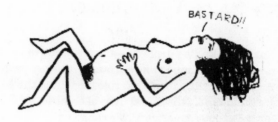

The Church has opposed every innovation and discovery from the day of Galileo down to our own time, when the use of anaesthetics in childbirth was regarded as a sin because it avoided the biblical curse pronounced against eve.
— Mark Twain

"He (Tinky- Winky) is purple, the gay pride colour;
and his antenna is shaped like a triangle, the gay pride
symbol. As a Christian I feel that role modelling the gay
life style is damaging the moral lives of children"
— Dr Jerry Falwell (American TV evangelist)

"There is not one verse in the bible inhibiting slavery, but many regulating it. It is not then, we conclude, immoral"
— Rev. Alex Cambell

The truths of religion are never so well understood as by those who have lost the power of reasoning
— Voltaire

Someone has to draw a line!

"LINE DANCING IS AS SINFUL AS ANY OTHER TYPE OF DANCING, WITH ITS SEXUAL GESTURES AND TOUCHING! IT IS AN INCITEMENT TO LUST!
— Dr Ian Paisley, Presbyterian minister and Northern Irish politician

Say what you will about the sweet miracle of unquestioning faith, I consider the capacity for it terrifying!
— Kurt Vonnegut Jr

ART

Art raises its head when religions relax their hold.
— Nietszche, F

Art makes the sight of life bearable by laying over it the veil of unclear thinking.
— Nietszche, F

Most art is useless, but it looks good after the moral question has faded.

For millennia morality has been thought of in terms of aesthetics. This basically meant that ideas of beauty and ideas of being good were woven together, i.e. good people were handsome. This would obviously create some problems for people who were not very dashing. A way to try and get around 'appearances' was to try imagining a realm that exists outside of our sense experiences. Maybe over there, judgements could be made that are universal and can exist independently of the existence of one person. The main protagonist for this type of thinking was Plato who was on Earth around 500 B.C. Now he exists independent of his body, and was everpresent in the minds of many a philosopher.

Establishing these principles that do not physically exist is being idealistic and rationalistic. Yearning for things is wrapped up in romanticism, which is greatly invigorating in the arts, but as a political philosophy, is a little problematic (Think about Fascism in Germany and Italy).

Pushing for great, glorious, unreachable goals does not go down very well at the average human level. Almost every 'big' philosopher has written about art but none of them were actually 'makers of things'. Nietzsche brings this point up, in regards to Kant's thoughts on beauty.

A distinction between art and morality is worth making, but at the moment we are not quite sure whether we want to follow a set of 'moral laws' supposedly laid down by some abstract Platonic force.

And Art, well, that's just another word, like Morality.

I spit upon beauty and those who fruitlessly admire it,
whensoever it causes no pleasure.
— Epicurus

... and I do not call any irrational activity an art.
— Plato

... for that kind of superiority must rest on greatness, just as personal beauty requires that one should be tall; little people may have charm and elegance, but beauty – no.
— Aristotle Nichomachean Ethics: Beauty of size

In the end the sorriest craftsman is still a maker of forms, ungracefully
— Plotinus

The fox knows many things, but the hedgehog knows one big thing.
— Archilochus

... in the mere state of nature, if you have a mind to kill, that state itself affords you a right.
— Thomas Hobbes

I have no knowledge of myself as I am, but merely as I appear to myself.
— Immanuel Kant

War, if it is carried on with order and with a sacred respect for the rights of citizens, has something sublime in it, and makes the disposition of the people who carry it on thus, only the more sublime, the more numerous are the dangers to which they are exposed, and in respect of which they behave with courage.
— Immanuel Kant

Now I say: the beautiful is the symbol of the morally good.
— Immanuel Kant

For beautiful art, therefore, imagination, understanding, spirit and taste are requisite. Taste is the faculty of judging an object or a method of representing it by an entirely disinterested satisfaction or dissatisfaction. The object of such satisfaction is called beautiful.
— Immanuel Kant

Kant, like all philosophers, instead of viewing the aesthetic issue from the side of the artist, envisaged art and beauty solely from the spectator's point of view, and so, without himself realising it, smuggled the 'spectator' into the concept of beauty... "That is beautiful", Kant proclaims, "which gives us disinterested pleasure" Disinterested! ... when our aestheticians tirelessly rehearse, in support of Kant's view, that the spell of beauty enables us to view even nude female statues 'disinterestedly' we may be allowed to laugh a little at their expense. The experiences of artists in this delicate matter are rather more 'interesting'.
— Friedrich Nietzsche

The beautiful exists just as little as the good, the true.
— Friedrich Nietzsche

Our religion, morality, and philosophy are decadent forms of man. The countermovement: art.
— Friedrich Nietzsche

When one has dealings with scholars and artists it
is easy to miscalculate in opposite directions: behind
a remarkable scholar one not infrequently finds a
mediocre man, and behind a mediocre artist often
– a very remarkable man.
— Friedrich Nietzsche

That which is done out of love always takes place beyond
good and evil.
— Friedrich Nietzsche

Art, like morality, consists in drawing the line
somewhere.
— G.K.Chesterton

Experience, it is said, makes a man wise. That is very silly talk. If there was nothing beyond experience it would drive him mad.
— Soren Kierkegaard

A highly embroiled quarter, a network of streets that I had avoided for years, was disentangled at a single stroke when one day a person dear to me moved there. It was as if a search light set up at this person's window dissected this area with pencils of light.
— Walter Benjamin

SEX

Philosophers have only interpreted the sexual act, the point is to change it. The political problem of sex is that politicians can no longer indulge in it without the masses noticing. Sex without morality is like breakfast without the morning paper. In philosophy sex is like the music of numbers, most philosophers can hum in an orderly fashion but they don't know the tune.

Sex and Morality are completely inseperable affairs. You could liken the situation to that of women and chocolate: In theory you would think that one could exist without the other, whereas in practice, you just know it wouldn't work. If PMT didn't exist, poor old Mr. Cadbury would be consigned to a two-bedroomed semi. Which, lets face it, is never going to happen! Sex without morality? Sounds like quite a tempting idea, but you just know that it will never happen. We are going to have to resign ourselves to guilt, shame, envy, jealousy, perversion and the like.

(NOT)

"We are never misunderstood, we are just sometimes understood in ways we don't like. We are never unfaithful, just sometimes faithful in ways we don't like."
— Adam Phillips

We are born into the middle of a labyrinth where a thousand turns are laid out for the sole purpose of leading us astray.
— Denis Diderot.

Whether monogamous, committing adultery, partaking in a one-night-stand or prostituting the body, we always stumble over messy complications and implications that come part and parcel with the dirty deed.

"Fitzjames Stephen, the nineteenth century philosopher of law, stated that 'the criminal law stands to the passion of revenge in the same relation as marriage to the sexual appetite'. Unfortunately he died without specifying the relation."
— Andrea Dworkin

"Infidelity is such a problem because we take monogamy for granted; we treat it as the norm. Perhaps we should take infidelity for granted, assume it with unharrassed ease. Then we would be able to think of monogamy"
— Adam Phillips

"Saturday 25th February 6pm

Oh joy. Have spent the day in a state I can only describe as shag-drunkenness, mooning about the flat. It was so lovely. The only down points were 1) immediately it was over Daniel said, 'Damn. I meant to take the car into the Citroen garage', and 2) when I got up to go to the bathroom he pointed out that I had a pair of tights stuck to the back of my calf. But as the rosy clouds begin to disperse, I begin to feel alarm. What now? No plans were made. Suddenly I realize I am waiting for the phone again. How can it be that the situation between the sexes after a first night remains so agonizingly imbalanced"
— Helen Fielding — Bridget Jones's Diary

There is always this recurring problem with partners. They insist on making sex more complicated that it need be. Perhaps if it were redesigned, the inventors of sex might come to the conclusion that sex should be like solitaire, a one manned thing (or indeed, a one womaned thing), here will be the Woody Allen quote about wanking...but I forgot how it goes, so somebody will have to fill it in for me!!

"I have noted with what disgusted scepticism prostitutes regard the respectable gentlemen who condemn vice in general but view their own personal whims with indulgence; yet they regard the girls who live off their bodies as perverted and debauched, not the males who use them... Woman plays the part of those secret agents who are left to the firing squad if they get caught, and are loaded with rewards if they succeed; it is for her to shoulder all man's immorality."
— Simone de Beauvoir

"She appears to the male as a sexual being...she is defined and differentiated with reference to her; she is the incidental, the inessential as opposed to the essential. He is the Subject, he is the Absolute - she is the Other."
— Simone de Beauvoir

Morality consists in suspecting other people of not being legally married
— George Bernard Shaw

There's sex, and then there is the public view of sex. Everybody loves it, but nobody wants you to talk about it (or maybe they do, if they're not getting enough). Speaking about sex in civil company, say for example over dinner with friends, is not exactly an accepted as the norm; "The weather's been great recently, shame I can't say the same about my husband's love-making' or even, 'this banana split looks fantastic, dear; really reminds me of ...' Yeah ... you get the drift!

She had made it impossible for my children to stay in their own house. It was the way she'd behaved around them: smoking at the breakfast table with her dressing gown not done up properly, her udderly breasts lolling around. The way she'd laughed that time she sat down and her vagina made a large squelchy noise; we could have all pretended not to have heard it but no, she had to make a fuss: 'Ha ha, fanny farts, Jo. Don't you just love them?' and she'd gone on about going to yoga class, and every time the teacher had lifted her leg, 'Her fanny would fart like Japanese fire crackers.'
— Jenny Eclair

The single life is the easiest antidote to all sexual problems, except of course repression! But this is far outweighed by the problems that couples have to deal with: loyalty, compromise, arguments, etc. I have enough trouble dealing with my own bad moods, let alone having to put up with somebody else's.

"If we could find a cure for sexual jealousy — perhaps a drug — what would we not be capable of? We would certainly have to rethink our ideas about progress. Or at the very least our ideas about progress in the arts."
— Adam Phillips

"A couple is a conspiracy in search of a crime. Sex is often the closest they can get."
— Adam Phillips

The sin, then, consists not in desiring a woman, but in
consent to the desire, and not the wish for whoredom,
but the consent to the wish is damnation.
— Alibard's Ethics

The degree and kind of a man's sexuality extends to the
highest pinnacle of his spirit.
— Nietzsche

In conceiving a recognizable injury from the viewpoint of the reasonable rapist, the rape law affirmatively rewards men with acquitals for not comprehending women's point of view on sexual encounters.
— Catherine A.MacKinnon

Desire is an attitude aiming at enchantment.
— Sartre

It seems most unlikely that so much effort would have been put into making women artificially dependant on men if they had been naturally so.
— Janet Radcliffe Richards

Women need men like a fish needs its fingers.
— Bjork

FREEDOM

Freedom can only be granted to those who refuse it. My freedom eats away my freedom. Man is condemned to be free. There is no such thing as a free lunch, only a free life.

LUCK

Moral luck occurs when luck makes a moral difference
to a person's life, changing either their moral status
in society, or their moral responsibility. Luck is the
fundamental factor that makes us who we are, where
we are and what we are. Luck cannot be manipulated,
or controlled in any way, and our good or bad fortune
is, therefore, brought about by the force of chance.
Everything in our lives has a direct, or indirect
occurrence from luck, whether we consciously or
unconsciously realise this, from the circumstances
we're born into, and the positions we end up in due
to all the intricate encounters with different people,
places, situations and circumstances. Experiences
develop our minds and manipulate our reactions,
constantly changing our responses over time. Because
very little of our life is under our control, it is hard to
see the fairness of holding anyone responsible for
anything. However, an individual's moral responsibility
plays a big part on society's stage, controlled by
punishment and revenge to achieve the moral 'good',
and there would be major problems if it was made
redundant. Morality, on the other hand, is something
man has invented and needs to keep under his control.

A man and a woman fell deeply in love. They were soul mates, both beautiful and intelligent, and believed they were meant to be together... Apart from the fact that her arms were slightly too short for his liking, and men with bent noses were something she normally avoided, everything was absolutely perfect... However, soon after their marriage, he discovered, whilst looking through old photographs, that she had an identical twin sister, identical in every way, apart from having just slightly longer arms, and who always fancied men with bent noses. He hadn't known anything about this woman until then, and arranged to meet her without his wife's knowledge. When they met, she was perfect for him in every way. He divorced his wife, and now lives happily with her sister in Margate, they have two kids and a dog called Scruff. His divorced wife killed herself after a nervous break-down linked to the break-up circumstances. The question is, should Scruff's master be treated harshly in society, decreasing his moral status, even though his situation was purely governed by luck?

The Dice Man, apparently a true story lived by the throw of the die. He chose his six chances time and again, and allowed luck to determine him. He proves that although we can't control luck, we can instigate the chance of something happening.

"He who is diceman truly lives"
— http://www.algonet.se/-kajn/wwwboard/wwwboard.htm

"Tremble in my hands, O Die, As I so shake in yours"
— Luke Rhinehart — The Dice Man

UGH!
BEANS FOR
TEA AGAIN

"da bone dice decide no bad"
— Matzu at above website

To use the die to determine everything you do is to consciously know no longer who you are.

If you had only enough money to buy and feed two budgerigars in a cage sufficient for no more, and the shop keeper sold you two males, of which one, unbeknown to you or the shop keeper was pregnant, could you be held morally responsible for the death of the offspring due to overcrowding and under nourishment?

CHANCE:

A possibility, an opportunity; a degree of likelihood
Development of events without planning or obvious
reason unplanned, happened by chance.

— Hurricane Katrina

— The universe

LUCK:

Good or bad fortune; chance thought of as a force
bringing this.

— Winning a holiday in New Orleans

— Finding oil in the desert

Surely we should only hold people morally responsible for things that happen under their control, but there is very little in a persons life that is under their control. If therefore we do hold them responsible for only that which is controlled by them, then we will not be holding them responsible for much. After scrutiny of this paradox, can we not almost eliminate responsibility altogether?

Prior to reflection it is intuitively plausible that people cannot be morally assessed for what is not their fault, or for what is due to factors beyond their control.'
— Nagel, 1993

Where a significant aspect of what someone does depends on factors beyond his control, yet we continue to treat him in that respect as an object of moral judgement, it can be called moral luck.'
— Nagel, 1993

'The luck involved relates not to our moral condition but only to our image: it relates not to what we are but to how people (ourselves included) will regard us.'
— Rescher, 1993

'The erosion of moral judgement emerges not as the absurd consequence of an over-simple theory, but as a natural consequence of the ordinary idea of moral assessment, when it is applied in view of a more complete and precise account of the facts.'
— Nagel, 1993

Can luck make a moral difference? Nagel argues that it can. Example: There were two drunk drivers. One was unfortunate enough to kill a child that was playing in the wrong place at the wrong time. Should we judge the unfortunate driver more harshly than the fortunate driver; even though the only difference between the two was that the unfortunate driver was faced with a circumstance beyond his control?

You make your own luck.
— Billy the Kid

BEING (MORAL) AND NOTHINGNESS

Football is the essence both of being, and nothingness, a true dialectic of triviality.

If God didn't exist, he would have had to invent us in order to invent him.

There are times when even to live is an act of bravery.
— Seneca

As a collection of DNA and nerve cell endings we do wonders with the fact of our utter irrelevance in the universe.

Man is the measure of all things.
— Protogoras

The most important human endeavor is the striving for morality in our actions. Our inner balance and even our very existence depend on it. Only morality in our actions can give beauty and dignity to life.
— Albert Einstein.

In history we developed, first there was art, then there was music, then there was Ozzie Osbourne.

Parents, teach your children to express themselves.
Teach them to be in touch with their emotions, to speak
honestly to people, and to maintain integrity and stick
by their principles in all they do. This is perhaps the
highest morality you can instill. But don't expect them
to succeed in business.
— Jeffrey Bryant

The truth is rarely pure and never simple, only people
are like that.

Morality is the best of all devices for leading mankind by
the nose
— Fredereich Neitszche

For over two thousand years it has been the custom
among earnest moralists to decry happiness as
something degraded and unworthy
— Bertrand Russell

Fear is the mother of morality
— Friedrich Nietzsche

In the beginning there was morality and then there were
lawyers.

Postscript

Kant, the great philosopher, tried to produce universal and scientific laws about morality, which led him into very complicated and technical areas of philosophy, and also into rather silly positions like 'under no circumstances whatever tell a lie'.

If someone knocks at your door and says 'I want to murder your wife is she in?' you are supposed to say 'Oh yes of course come in.' Now you may have said this because she was really annoying you, or because you were very, very honest, or because you had paid someone to murder her, but the fact of telling the truth isn't the same as doing a sensible moral thing. If you just say 'No she's out' that'll be the end of that.

The Karmic notion that bad actions will follow you around is rather a good moral principle, but also may not be true. Whichever way you look at it acting morally is a very complicated business, and gets more complicated all the time.

This is not to say that any morality will do but that defining how one can be moral in a deeply amoral world is much harder than it appears. That is probably why self-interest has come to be such a dominant approach; for one thing it is simple. 'I'll do what I feel like' doesn't take all that much thinking about. As someone once said 'The difference between good and evil is that they are spelt differently.'

However we'll leave it with Plato who said:

'No one does wrong willingly'!

Some things to read if you want to take it further

Beck, John E *Morality and Citizenship* (1998)

Benjamin Greenwood Gregg *Morality and Law* (2005)

Dostoevsky, F *Crime and Punishment* (any edition)

Fein, Melvyn L *Race and Morality* (2001)

Held, Virginia *Feminist Morality: Transforming Culture, Society, and Politics* (1993)

Hondereich, Ted *After the Terror* (2002)

Hornby, Nick *How to be Good* (2003)

Holloway, Richard *Godless Morality: Keeping Religion Out of Ethics* (2002)

Koestler, A *Darkness at Noon* (any edition)

McCall Smith, Alexander *Morality for Beautiful Girls* (2003)

Martin, Micheal *Atheism, Morality and Meaning* (2002)

Midgely, Mary *Wickedness* 2006

Scheffler, Samuel *Human Morality* (1992)

Sherba, James et al. *Morality and Social Justice* (1995)

Silverstone, Roger *Media and Morality* (2006)

Spinello Richard A *Cyberethics: Morality and Law in Cyberspace* (2002)

Taylor, Charles *The Morality Police* (2001)

Wilson, James Q *The Moral Sense* (1997)